BE YOUR OWN
ASTRONOMY
EXPERT

Guillaume Cannat
Nathalie Locoste, Jean-Claud

Sterling Publishing Co., Inc.   New York

Text by Guillaume Cannat
Illustrated by Nathalie Locoste and Jean-Claude Senée
Translated by Fay Greenbaum; English edition edited by Isabel Stein

Library of Congress Cataloging-in-Publication Data

Cannat, Guillaume.
    [Construis ta station d'astronomie. English]
    Be your own astronomy expert / Guillaume Cannat, Nathalie Locoste & Jean-Claude Senée.
        p.   cm.
    Includes index.
    Summary: Provides information about the earth, moon, sun, stars, and other astronomical phenomena, presenting facts, folklore, and activities.
    ISBN 0-8069-6131-7
    1. Astronomy—Juvenile literature. [1. Astronomy. 2. Solar system.]
I. Locoste, Nathalie. II. Senée, Jean-Claude.
QB46.C2813 1996
520—dc20

          96-26123
          CIP
          AC

10 9 8 7 6 5 4 3 2 1

Published in 1996 by Sterling Publishing Company, Inc.
387 Park Avenue South, New York, N.Y. 10016
First published in France by Éditions Mango
under the title *Construis Ta Station d'Astronomie*
© 1993 by Éditions Mango
English translation © 1996 by Sterling Publishing Company
Distributed in Canada by Sterling Publishing
% Canadian Manda Group, One Atlantic Avenue, Suite 105
Toronto, Ontario, Canada M6K 3E7
Printed in Hong Kong
All rights reserved

Sterling ISBN 0-8069-6131-7

CONTENTS

DISCOVER ASTRONOMY

Can you find the constellation Ursa Major, the Big Bear? Have you ever watched the Sun set? The sky is full of unusual and beautiful objects, which you can find easily: All you have to do is go away from a big city, which is too illuminated and has too much air pollution, and look up. The Sun, the Moon, and the planets are as much a part of your environment as trees and animals are, but getting to know them will take you on a much longer journey.

WHAT IS ASTRONOMY?

Astronomers study heavenly bodies that you can see with your eyes alone, like the Moon and the Sun, and also those that are not visible except with special instruments (binoculars or telescopes). Astronomers try to understand how stars are formed, why life appeared on Earth and not on Mars, where galaxies come from.... Thanks to rocket ships, probes can be sent into space in search of planets, and telescopes can be placed in orbit around the Earth in order to operate away from air pollution.

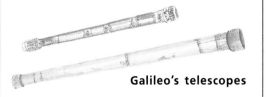

Galileo's telescopes

THE STARS
pages 32–37

THE SUN
pages 22–25

GET READY TO
WATCH THE SKY
pages 14–15

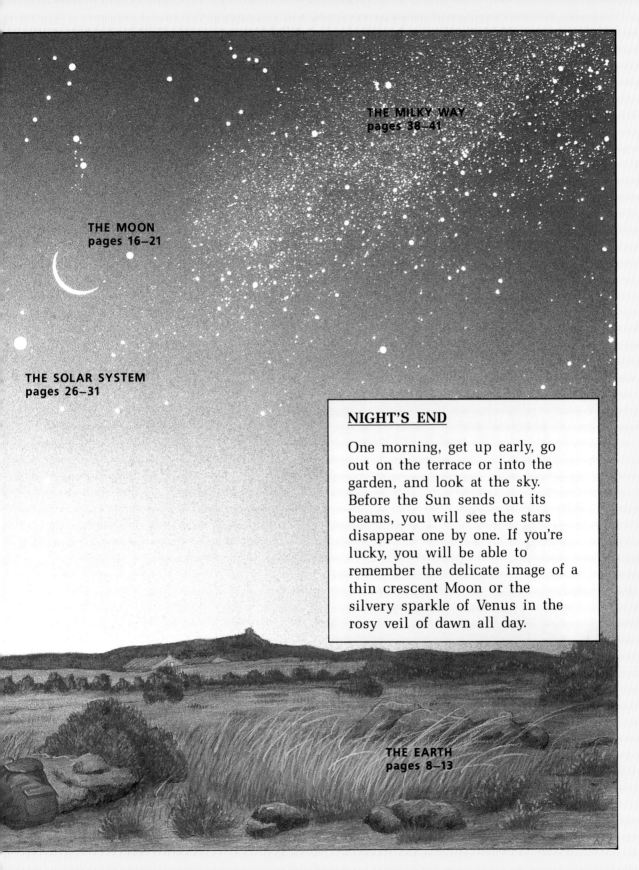

THE MILKY WAY
pages 38–41

THE MOON
pages 16–21

THE SOLAR SYSTEM
pages 26–31

NIGHT'S END

One morning, get up early, go out on the terrace or into the garden, and look at the sky. Before the Sun sends out its beams, you will see the stars disappear one by one. If you're lucky, you will be able to remember the delicate image of a thin crescent Moon or the silvery sparkle of Venus in the rosy veil of dawn all day.

THE EARTH
pages 8–13

THE EARTH

Perhaps you have seen a picture of the Earth on television during the weather report. It is a beautiful round, blue planet, surrounded by a fine atmosphere in which clouds float. It is a little like a spaceship that carries us along on its annual path around the Sun.

THE EARTH IS ROUND

At the seashore, watch a boat through binoculars as it moves into the distance. You will see first the hull, then the sail, and finally the top of the mast disappear at the horizon. If the Earth were flat, you would see the whole boat at the horizon.

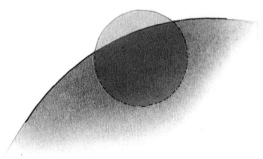

The shadow of an object always has about the same shape as the object. Look at the shape of the Earth's shadow on the Moon during a lunar eclipse; it is round.

For the Mayas, the Earth was square and rested on the back of an immense, swimming tortoise. Four gigantic trees supported a dome prickled with stars.

The ancient Greeks thought the Earth was flat and that it was at the center of a double sphere filled with fire. They believed the stars were little holes through which people could see the fire.

HOW BIG IS IT?

More than 2200 years ago
Eratosthenes estimated the
diameter of the Earth at 7200 mi
(12 000 km). The actual diameter is
7654 mi (12 756 km) at the equator
and a little less if measured at the
poles (7628 mi or 12 713 km), as
the Earth is very slightly flattened.

Since the 1970s, satellites have been
continuously photographing the Earth.
Seen from outer space, continents are
brown, oceans are blue, and ice and
clouds are white. Astronauts say that
the big cities are so lit up at night
that they can be seen from outer
space. What impressed them the most
is how thin the atmosphere is: it
seems no thicker than a sheet of
cigarette paper sitting on an orange!

DAY AND NIGHT

Take an orange, representing Earth, and pierce it through with a knitting needle. Then make a mark on it with a black felt-tip pen. Go into a dark room. Place your orange near a lamp (representing the Sun), as shown here: your mark should be lit up. If you rotate the orange gently, your mark will pass into the shadow; for that mark it's nighttime. Keep turning the orange and your mark will come back into the light; day is breaking!

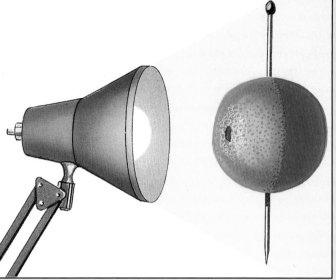

THE EARTH ROTATES ABOUT ITSELF

The Earth is a little like your orange. It rotates about itself every 24 hours. Because the Earth turns, we have day and night. The rooster and the kangaroo, shown in the drawing below, pass round and round into the shadow (night) and into the light (day). You can see the length of the day (in red) and of the night (in black) for these two animals; the rooster's day is much longer than that of the kangaroo. (For the night, it's exactly the opposite.) What season do you think it is for the rooster? For the kangaroo?

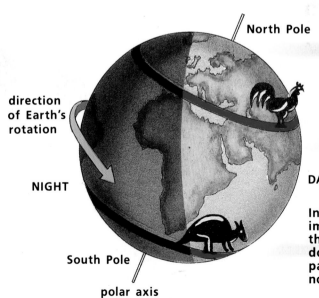

North Pole

direction of Earth's rotation

NIGHT

DAY

South Pole

polar axis

the Sun's rays

In reality, the "knitting needle" (the imaginary axis that passes through the poles) is not straight up and down, but tilted in relation to Earth's path. Without this tilt there would be no seasons.

10

AT THE POLES

The Earth rotates about itself on an axis that links the north pole (NP) with the south pole (SP). This axis of rotation is tilted, and it is because of this inclination that the polar regions have a special situation: for six months it is continually night; then for six months it is continually day.

At the equator. The equator is equally distant from each pole. In the equatorial region, day and night are the same length all year long: 12 hours. It is always summer.

path of the Earth around the Sun

THE MIDNIGHT SUN

When it is summer in Europe and North America, as in the drawing on the opposite page, the north pole is inclined toward the Sun. The Sun never sets at all over the arctic lands; it appears to travel across the sky for 24 hours!

THE SUN DOES NOT TRAVEL AROUND THE EARTH

It appears to us that the Sun rises in the morning, crosses the sky, and sets in the evening, after traveling in a semicircle. In reality, the Sun does not travel. The Earth, rotating about itself, causes the Sun to appear to rise, move across the sky, and then set.

THE SEASONS

Imagine the Sun and the Earth sitting on an immense ice skating rink. Our planet rotates about itself at the same time as it glides around the Sun. The Earth is a little like a skater who is always bent at the same angle to the ice. In figure 1 below, the northern hemisphere is tilted towards the Sun; six months later (figure 2), it is the southern hemisphere that is tilted towards the Sun. The more a hemisphere is tilted towards the Sun, the higher the Sun appears to climb in the sky during the day. In consequence, the Sun's course is longer and day lasts longer.

In New York City, in the month of June, the Sun rises to a maximum height of 73°, and the day lasts about 15 hours. Six months later, in December, the Sun's maximum height is 27° and it remains in the sky for only 9 hours (see p. 25). It is exactly the reverse in the southern hemisphere.

THE MOVEMENT OF THE EARTH AROUND THE SUN

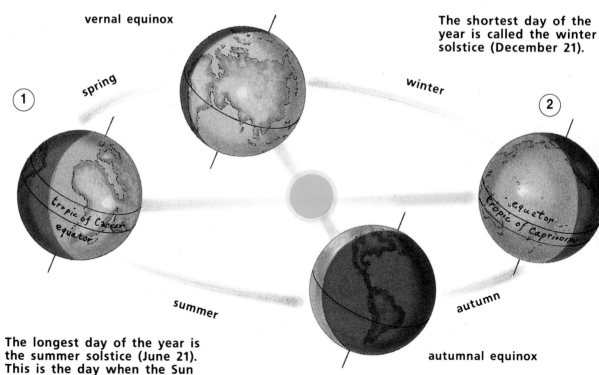

vernal equinox

spring

The shortest day of the year is called the winter solstice (December 21).

winter

① ②

tropic of Cancer
equator

equator
tropic of Capricorn

summer

autumn

autumnal equinox

The longest day of the year is the summer solstice (June 21). This is the day when the Sun appears to climb highest in the sky.

There are two times of the year when day and night last exactly the same amount of time all over the planet: the vernal and autumnal equinoxes.

The variation in hours of sunshine determines the passage from one season to another. Study the shadows; they are very long in winter and very short in summer.

Note the height of the Sun every day around noon (see p. 25). You will notice that the Sun is much higher in the sky in summer than in winter.

June 28 at 2 p.m. (local noon)

←20→ (7⅞")
cm

(see p. 25)

ABOUT THE DRAWINGS

The Earth is 110 times smaller in diameter than the Sun. So you can see it, Earth's size is greatly exaggerated in the drawing on p. 12. The distance between Earth and Sun is really much greater than shown.

the drawing on p. 12

THE CALENDAR

It is often said that a year lasts 365 days. But in one year, our planet makes 365.2422 rotations about itself. To correct this difference, astronomers have ordered a leap year, every four years, which includes a 366th day, February 29. But this average of 365.25 days for four years is a little too much. To reestablish the balance, one leap year is suppressed every hundred years, except when the first two numbers of the century are evenly divisible by 4. Thus, 1700, 1800 and 1900 only had 365 days, while the year 2000 will have 366 days. Finally, so that our calendar will be absolutely correct, one more leap year is removed every 3313 years; the first time will be in 4896!

THE HISTORY OF CLIMATE

By counting the number of annular rings in a cross-section of a felled tree, you will get its age (one ring = 1 year). Astronomers study the rings to reconstruct the climates of past centuries. If the ring is thin, the year was dry, and the tree did not grow much. Some fossilized trees found in the United States reveal what the climate was like 2000 or 3000 years ago, and so we can calculate whether the Sun always has shone the same way.

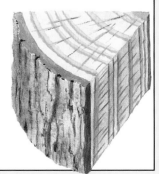

GET READY TO WATCH THE SKY

Let's plan an evening of star-gazing. You must choose a place to make your observations and prepare for your amazing journey through the heavens. Don't forget to put a vacuum bottle with a warm drink in your astronomer's bag, and remember to dress warmly. In summer as well as in winter, people get cold when they stay still for a long time, watching the Milky Way....

PROTECT YOUR EYES

If you go from a brightly lit room to a dark room, your eyes need a certain amount of time to adapt to the darkness and see objects. Likewise, if you go out at night to study the sky, you have to wait a few minutes before you can locate the fainter stars. If a very strong light (for example, a street lamp or headlights) interrupts your sky watch, you will have to wait a few minutes before being able see the stars in the night sky again.

CHOOSE A GOOD LOCATION

Avoid roadsides and parking lots so your eyes won't be dazzled by headlights and street lamps. A courtyard or garden surrounded by trees will do if you live in the city. In the country, it is better to pick a meadow, so you can see the stars appear on the eastern horizon.

Go with friends and don't go too far from home, as you may need to return from time to time to get warm. Don't forget to tell your parents where your observation site is.

To find the direction of your observations, you will need a small map of the sky.

Northern Hemisphere   Southern Hemisphere

SUPPLIES AND ADVICE

Take lightweight binoculars (field glasses) to observe the planets or the Moon (but not the Sun). Binoculars that enlarge 6 to 8 times are perfect.

Certain foods aid your night vision. For this reason, airplane pilots and astronomers regularly eat carrots and blueberry jam.

At night, you need red lamp for light that won't interfere with your night vision. Paint the bulb of a flashlight with red nail polish to make one.

Useful things to take: a pad for taking notes, a sky map, a blanket, a snack, and a vacuum bottle holding something warm to drink.

THE MOON

It is round, it circles the Earth, and people have gone to visit it.... It's the Moon, of course. Some evenings, you can see it sporting its prettiest crescent; at other times it is all round and fills the night with a pale light. Let's explore the Earth's only natural satellite.

THE EARTH'S SATELLITE

How was the Moon formed? One theory is that 4.5 billion years ago (4.5 x 10⁹ years ago), the Earth collided with a small planet. From the violence of the shock, a part of the Earth's surface was thrown into the sky. Little by little, the remains of the small planet and the debris from the Earth got stuck together to give birth to the Moon. This natural satellite has circled our planet since then in a somewhat bizarre fashion; its orbit looks more like an ellipse than a circle.

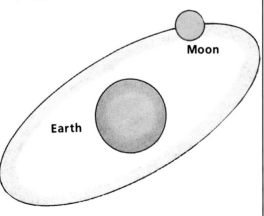

STARS IN DAYLIGHT

What do you notice in this picture? The ground is lit by the Sun, so it is day, but you can see stars in the black sky. On Earth, stars are invisible in daylight because the Sun illuminates the atmosphere. But on the Moon, there is no atmosphere; as a consequence, the sky is always black, and we can watch the stars 24 hours a day. It is a paradise for astronomers, who hope—among other things—to one day put an observatory on the Moon.

The Moon has no inhabitants. The twelve men who walked on the Moon between 1969 and 1972 are the only "Moonmen" so far.

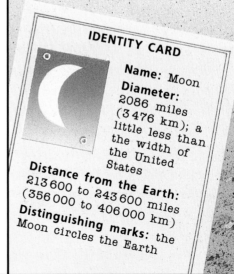

IDENTITY CARD

Name: Moon
Diameter: 2086 miles (3476 km); a little less than the width of the United States
Distance from the Earth: 213 600 to 243 600 miles (356 000 to 406 000 km)
Distinguishing marks: the Moon circles the Earth

In the Moon's sky, astronauts admire a crescent Earth. Since the Earth is 3.5 times as large as the Moon, Earth's crescent is 3.5 times bigger than the little crescent of the Moon you see from your house.

The Moon is a large stone sphere without atmosphere (air), and it is very cold on the part that is turned away from the Sun and very hot on the part that is getting sunlight. To breathe and keep warm, astronauts wear heated space suits equipped with oxygen tanks.

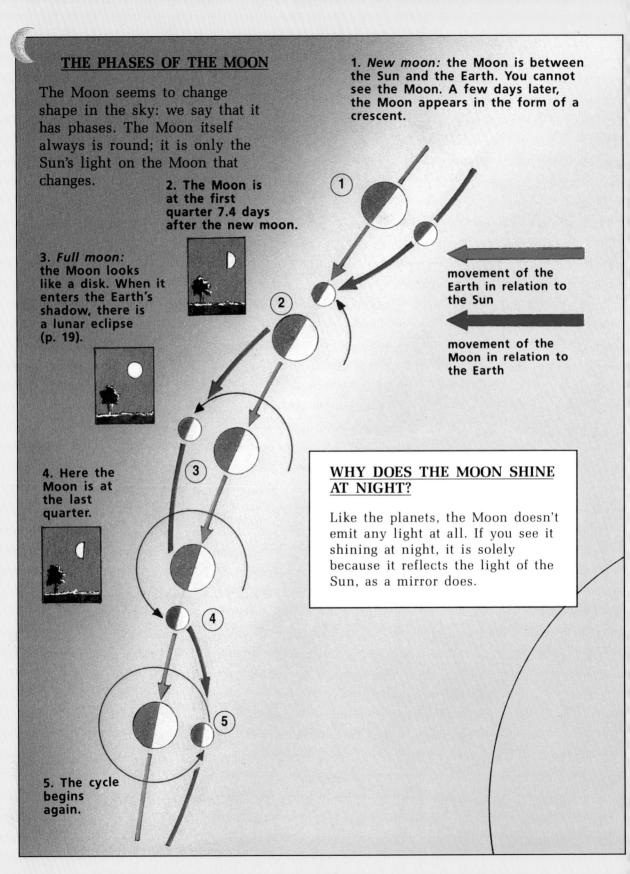

THE PHASES OF THE MOON

The Moon seems to change shape in the sky: we say that it has phases. The Moon itself always is round; it is only the Sun's light on the Moon that changes.

1. *New moon:* the Moon is between the Sun and the Earth. You cannot see the Moon. A few days later, the Moon appears in the form of a crescent.

2. The Moon is at the first quarter 7.4 days after the new moon.

3. *Full moon:* the Moon looks like a disk. When it enters the Earth's shadow, there is a lunar eclipse (p. 19).

4. Here the Moon is at the last quarter.

5. The cycle begins again.

movement of the Earth in relation to the Sun

movement of the Moon in relation to the Earth

WHY DOES THE MOON SHINE AT NIGHT?

Like the planets, the Moon doesn't emit any light at all. If you see it shining at night, it is solely because it reflects the light of the Sun, as a mirror does.

ALWAYS THE SAME SIDE

Day after day, whatever the Moon's phase, you always see the same side of the Moon. However, the Moon rotates about itself, just like the Earth. It takes the same amount of time to spin, or rotate, once on its axis as it does to orbit the Earth. With the help of a friend, you can simulate the movement of the Moon around the Earth (as shown in the drawing).

You always see the same side of the Moon in the sky. But don't worry; the photos brought back by the Apollo astronauts show the hidden side of the Moon.

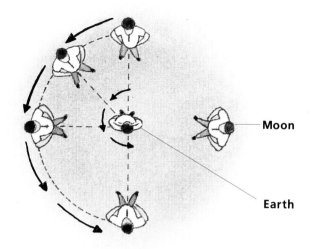

Moon

Earth

The Moon rotates about itself in 27 days, 7 hours, and 43 minutes. It circles the Earth in the same time.

LUNAR ECLIPSE

The Earth circles the Sun, and the Moon circles the Earth. This celestial trio occasionally offers us exceptional shows: eclipses. The Moon regularly passes into

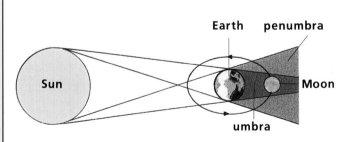

Earth   penumbra

Sun

Moon

umbra

the shadow of the Earth, and then it doesn't get any direct light from the Sun. During the eclipse, the Moon seems reddish for one or two hours. You can observe this phenomenon without binoculars.

0 hour: the Moon is full. It moves into the penumbra (semidarkness).

+1 hour: the Moon is in the penumbra of the Earth. It is gray.

+3 hours: the Moon is no longer visible. It is in the Earth's full shadow (umbra).

+5 hours: the end of the eclipse. The Moon is full.

BUILD A TELESCOPE

MATERIALS

2 sheets of flexible cardboard

two magnifying glasses of very different magnifications (2 times and 8 times)

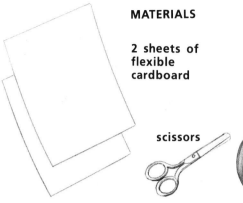

scissors

tape

tape measure

1. Take the magnifying glass with the lower magnification* and measure its focal length—the distance between the magnifying glass and the smallest point of light.

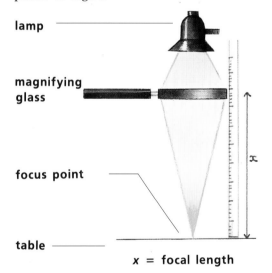

lamp

magnifying glass

focus point

table

x = focal length

2. Subtract 2 inches (5 cm) from the focal length (x). Measure off x − 5 cm (or x − 2 inches) on the length of each of the cardboard sheets and cut the length to that measure.

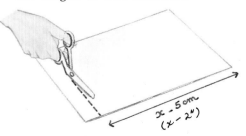

3. Bend the cardboards and tape them to make two tubes of different diameters so that one can slide into the other. Adjust them around your magnifying glasses and tape them in place.

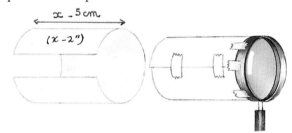

4. Gently put the two tubes together and make sure they slide together and apart easily. If they do not, you can glue pieces of felt to the small tube in order to get more consistent friction.

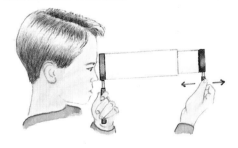

5. Choose an object fairly far away and focus on it by moving the small tube forward or backward. When the image is clear, you will notice that it is reversed. But for looking at the Moon or the stars, that's really not a problem!

*This one goes at the eye end of the telescope.

OBSERVE AND DRAW THE MOON

The surface of the Moon is sprinkled with grayish areas called *maria* (seas) and with immense craters, which you can see with binoculars or a telescope. One of the best ways to learn to recognize them is to draw them. Start by making two little sketches: one to locate the Moon in relation to the horizon of your sky watch site, the other to indicate precisely the lunar area you are going to draw. In the beginning, do not try to draw everything you see. Draw only the large formations (seas, craters). As you get more practice, you will be able to draw the craters one by one, with their shadows and their exact shapes; but for that, you will need a telescope with a magnification of at least 50 times (50 ×). There are maps of the Moon's surface to guide you.

Write down the date and hour you do your drawing; you will be able to follow your progress by leafing through your pad later on.

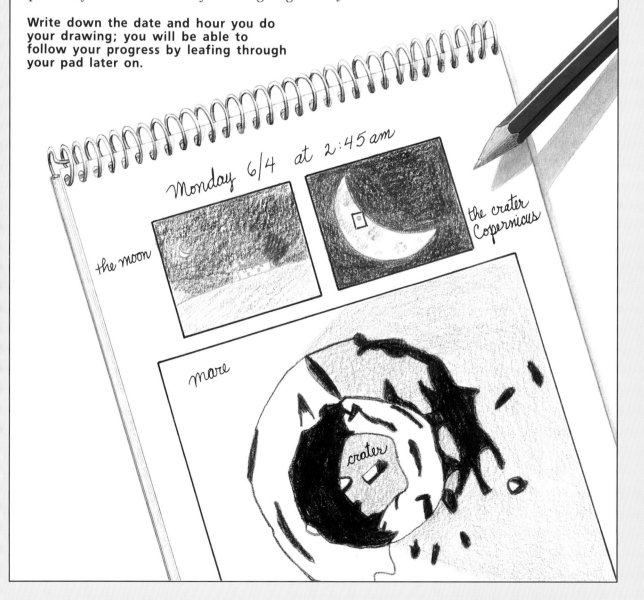

THE SUN

Without the Sun, there would be no life on Earth. Its rays bring warmth and light, and give rhythm to the seasons. But our Sun is just one of the thousands of stars you see at night. It is so important because it is very near us, while the other stars are very far away.

THE SUN IS A STAR

It is made up of very hot gases and it produces heat and light. Its core resembles a nuclear reactor; it is always burning and its temperature exceeds 14 million C° (14×10^6°C), while the surface reaches "only" 6000°C!

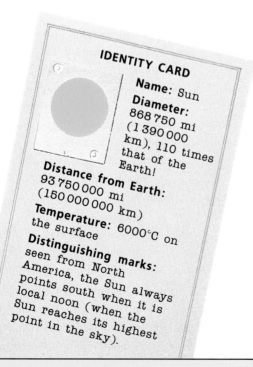

IDENTITY CARD

Name: Sun

Diameter: 868 750 mi (1 390 000 km), 110 times that of the Earth!

Distance from Earth: 93 750 000 mi (150 000 000 km)

Temperature: 6000°C on the surface

Distinguishing marks: seen from North America, the Sun always points south when it is local noon (when the Sun reaches its highest point in the sky).

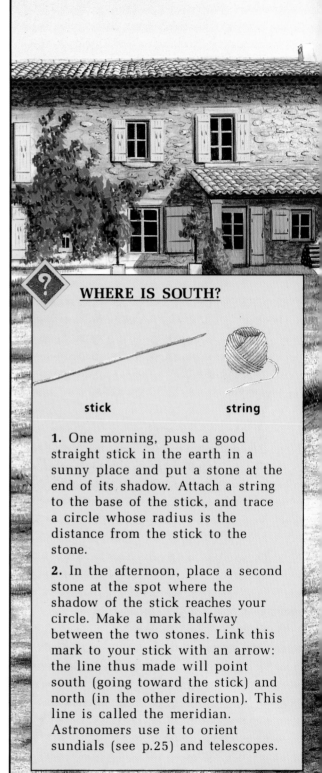

WHERE IS SOUTH?

stick   string

1. One morning, push a good straight stick in the earth in a sunny place and put a stone at the end of its shadow. Attach a string to the base of the stick, and trace a circle whose radius is the distance from the stick to the stone.

2. In the afternoon, place a second stone at the spot where the shadow of the stick reaches your circle. Make a mark halfway between the two stones. Link this mark to your stick with an arrow: the line thus made will point south (going toward the stick) and north (in the other direction). This line is called the meridian. Astronomers use it to orient sundials (see p.25) and telescopes.

WARNING!
Never look at the Sun with the naked eye, or through an instrument (binoculars, telescope); you risk burning your eyes.

Sun

south

north

WHAT IS AN ECLIPSE?

There are two kinds of eclipses:

• one celestial body hides another by passing in front of it. During an eclipse of the Sun, the Moon gets in between the Earth and the Sun and prevents the sunlight from reaching us.

• one celestial body passes into the shadow of another and disappears, as it is no longer lit by the Sun. During an eclipse of the Moon, the Moon is covered by the Earth's shadow.

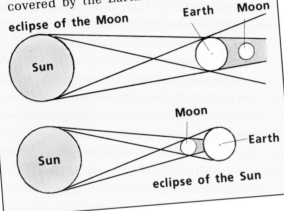

eclipse of the Moon

Sun · Earth · Moon

eclipse of the Sun

Sun · Moon · Earth

ECLIPSE OF THE SUN

When the Moon passes in front of the Sun, a solar eclipse can occur. The shadow of the Moon is round, but, because the Earth turns, a solar eclipse is visible in a strip several thousand kilometers long.

For inhabitants of regions crossed by the lunar shadow, the Sun disappears for a few minutes, and it becomes night in the middle of the day. Outside of the strip of totality (total eclipse), there is a partial eclipse, but generally, it is not noticeable because, even partially eclipsed, the Sun is still very bright.

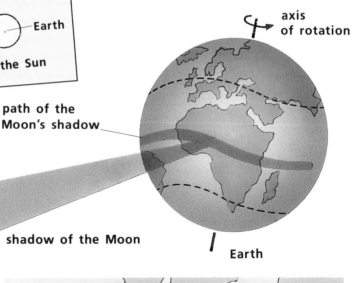

axis of rotation

path of the Moon's shadow

Moon

shadow of the Moon

Earth

Sun's rays

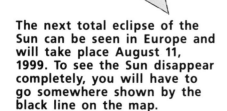

The next total eclipse of the Sun can be seen in Europe and will take place August 11, 1999. To see the Sun disappear completely, you will have to go somewhere shown by the black line on the map.

THE LENGTH OF SHADOWS

The length of a stick's shadow depends on the height of the Sun: the higher it is, the shorter the shadow. Plant a stick 39 in. (1 m) long at 90° to the ground and measure its shadow around noon. You will notice that the shadow is shortest in June, when the Sun is highest above the southern horizon, and longest in December, when the Sun is lowest at noon.

LENGTH OF A SHADOW AT LOCAL NOON

You can calculate the angle of the Sun's rays with a protractor

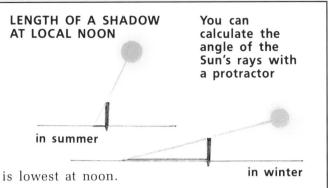

in summer

in winter

BUILD A SUNDIAL

MATERIALS

How a sundial works

The shadow of an object fixed to the Earth (a tree for example, or your stick) moves all the day long because, although the light source (the Sun) doesn't move, the Earth does. The Sundial is based on the principle of the movement of the shadow.

Assembly

1. Since the Earth makes one rotation around itself (360°) in 24 hours, we can calculate that it rotates 15° (360° ÷ 24) in an hour. Take a thick sheet of stiff cardboard and draw a circle on it. Using a protractor, divide it into 24 parts of 15° each, and number them from 1 to 24.

2. In the center of the circle, hammer a large nail, inclined at 45° toward 12 o'clock (north). Its shadow will tell you the solar time.

3. Orient your sundial so the nail is lined up along the meridian (see p. 22).

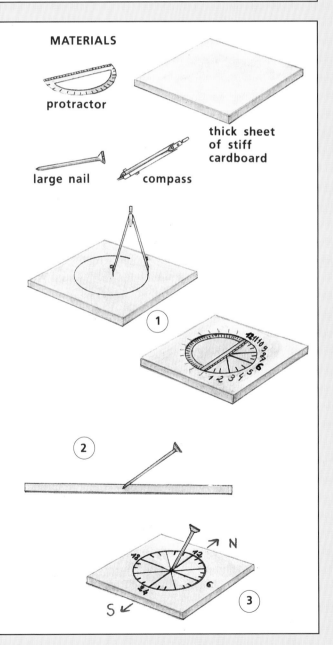

protractor

thick sheet of stiff cardboard

large nail   compass

THE SOLAR SYSTEM

Earth is not the only planet in our little solar system; there are eight others that circle the Sun. All except Mercury and Venus have one or several moons. These nine planets and their satellites, along with thousands of meteoroids, asteroids, and comets, circle the Sun and, with it, constitute the solar system.

DON'T CONFUSE PLANETS AND STARS

Some planets are made of rocks and some are mostly made up of gases. Stars are gigantic spheres of gas that are so hot that they are glowing. You can only see the planets because they are lit by the Sun, as they do not produce any light. Although people have lit their cities well, it is not enough to make the Earth shine on its own!

DID YOU KNOW?

From Earth you can observe solar and lunar eclipses. With a telescope, you can also see eclipses of Jupiter's moons, when they cover each other or disappear into the shadow of the immense planet.

One of Neptune's moons has an atmosphere

Jupiter is the largest planet in our solar system

It is very hot on Venus (485°C)

GASEOUS PLANETS

Jupiter, Saturn, Uranus, and Neptune are very large. Astronomers call them "gaseous planets" as they are made up of enormous clouds of gas, for the most part. Another peculiarity: they are surrounded by rings of dust and ice.

TERRESTRIAL PLANETS

Four little planets travel in orbits near the Sun: Mercury, Venus, Earth, and Mars. All have similar rocky surfaces; they are called terrestrial (earthlike) planets.

The rings of Saturn are visible through binoculars

Mercury is closest to the Sun

Earth is the only planet that supports life

Mars has a rust-colored surface

Uranus looks like a small greenish marble when seen through a telescope

Pluto, located at the outer limits of the solar system, is the smallest planet

OBSERVE THE PLANETS

You can observe the planets with the naked eye or through binoculars. Since the planets always move, they are not shown on star charts. To find them, you can study the sky and look for a bright object not on the chart, or watch the sky nightly or weekly, looking for the "wanderers."

Note in your pad, the day, hour, weather and the name of the planet you are observing.

Saturday July 24
— around 10:00 pm
— A beautiful clear sky.
— Saturn shining brightly toward the South.
— Venus set to the West, just after sunset.
— Jupiter not visible.

When you use a telescope, lean against a wall for stability.

ADJUST YOUR BINOCULARS

To adjust binoculars for your vision, start by looking at any bright star. Close your right eye and focus with the central focusing wheel; the image of the star should be as small as possible (like a dot). When it is clear for your left eye, open your right eye, close the left one, and correct the focus with the little focusing ring on the right eyepiece.

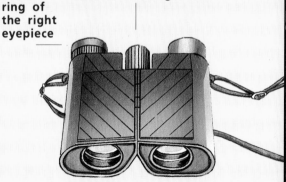

central focusing wheel

ring of the right eyepiece

BUILD A SCALE MODEL OF THE SOLAR SYSTEM

We are going to build two different models of the solar system: one model built to scale for distance, the other built to scale for size.

Scale model for distance

Materials: One string 65 feet (20 m) long, 10 ping-pong balls, a tape measure, cellophane tape, a yardstick.

Stretch out your string outdoors. At one end, tape a ball with the letter "S" for "Sun." Consult the table of distances (p.42) and label and attach the other balls corresponding to the planets at the correct distances from the Sun.

Scale model for size

Use the diameters given on page 42 to draw the planets in chalk on the ground.

What do you notice? The four terrestrial planets are really squeezed against the Sun (look at the pink line at the right). The planets that follow are further and further out; for them, the Sun is nothing but a particularly bright star at night.

Scale drawing for distances

S: Sun	5. Jupiter
1. Mercury	6. Saturn
2. Venus	7. Uranus
3. Earth	8. Neptune
4. Mars	9. Pluto

What do you notice? The Sun would be 45.5 feet (14 m) in diameter if you drew it; it is bigger than all the planets placed side to side.

OTHER HEAVENLY BODIES IN THE SOLAR SYSTEM

"Shooting star." Rub your hands together; they get warm! As debris from a comet (sand, rock fragments, frozen gases) passes through Earth's atmosphere, it heats up from the friction and melts, leaving behind it a beautiful illuminated trail. We call it a shooting star, but actually, it is a meteor.

Don't confuse meteors with comets; meteors are passing through Earth's atmosphere and barely last a second; comets are balls of dust and ice whose diameters reach several kilometers, which cross the sky in 2 or 3 weeks as they orbit the Sun.

Meteorite. When a meteor, a chunk of rock or metal from space, survives its journey through Earth's atmosphere and hits the Earth, it is known as a meteorite. It can make a crater when it hits the Earth.

The largest meteorite known weighs 60 metric tons. It was found in 1920 in South-West Africa.

Meteor Crater in Arizona measures ¾ mi. (1.2 km) in diameter and 650 ft. (200 m) deep.

Asteroids. These are heavenly bodies made of rock and metal, which circle the Sun like the planets, but are smaller than planets. They come in all sizes, from several yards (several meters) across to 600 mi. (1,000 km) across.

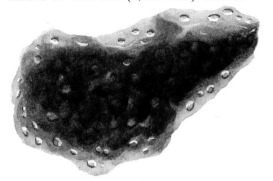

? OTHER PLANETS?

Astronomers are convinced that thousands of planets circling other stars in the universe exist, and they try to locate them. They have found several in the constellations of Pegasus, Ursa Major, and Virgo. As you saw on page 29, planets are very small relative to their star, and very often are close up to it. Seeing them is as difficult as noticing the glimmer of a candle before the blinding light of a beacon. If you want to become an astronomer, there are still many other things to discover in the sky.

BECOME A METEORITE HUNTER

MATERIALS

small knife

magnet

a very clean basin

1. Wait for the first rain after 12 August. Then put your basin outside.

2. After one hour, go get it and put it in a very dry and airy place. Don't touch it again until all of the water has evaporated.

3. If your hunt has been successful, you will find a bit of dust stuck to the bottom of the basin. Scrape it gently with your knife and bring the magnet close to it. Watch carefully: if you have gathered bits of meteorites, they will be drawn to the magnet, because they contain iron.

THE STARS

There are thousands of stars in the sky. They are grouped together in constellations such as Ursa Major, the Big Bear; Gemini, and Orion, named for a famous hunter in Greek mythology (middle drawing). In good conditions (in the mountains, for example) you can count up to 3,000 stars with the naked eye. In cities, you see fewer of them, because of pollution and electric lights.

DID YOU KNOW?

• The Sun is a star. It is the closest star to Earth. According to the scale of the model on page 29, the Sun is 19½ inches (50 cm) from Earth (which represents 93 million miles), while the star Proxima Centauri, the star closest to us after the Sun, would be at 88 miles (141 km) from Earth in the model.
• When you look at a constellation, you get the impression that the stars are near to each other. In reality, they are situated in the same direction, but not at the same depth in the sky (p. 37).
• You can see many double stars in the sky. Some of them rotate around each other, but more often, they are not the same distance from Earth.
• There are a total of 88 constellations, but from the Northern Hemisphere you can only see about 60 in a year.

CELESTIAL MYTHOLOGY

Since ancient times people have grouped the stars into constellations. All the bright stars in the same area were associated in their imagination to form a mythological character or animal. The Egyptians, the Chinese, the Mayas and many others came up with hundreds of different constellations. Today, many constellations have the names and shapes given them by the early Greeks and Romans; these names are used all over the world.

Draco, the Dragon, twines around near the north celestial pole and Polaris.

Proxima Centauri, the next closest star to us after the Sun, is located in the constellation of Centaurus, the Centaur.

MAKE A GAME OF SEVEN GROUPS OF CONSTELLATIONS

This game is a good way to learn the names of many constellations that may be seen in the skies of the northern hemisphere.

MATERIALS

colored markers

eraser

pencil

a sky map or a book with drawings of the constellations

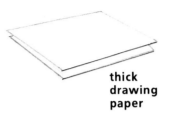

thick drawing paper

scissors

a ruler

Cut 35 rectangles, each 3½ × 2½ in. (8.5 × 5.5 cm), from the thick paper. Use a sky map or an astronomy book to help you draw one constellation in the center of each playing card. The list of groups of constellations for the game is given on page 43.

At the top of each card, use a felt-tip marker to write the name of the group

Carefully draw the shape of and the stars in the constellation.

At the bottom, write the name of the constellation you have drawn

HOW TO PLAY

Shuffle the 35 cards and deal 5 cards to each player (there can be 3 or 4 players); the remaining cards go in the pile. The first player requests a card from anyone; if he or she gets it, the player continues to play, if not, the player picks a card from the pile. If the pick is good, the player can once again request a card of whomever he or she wishes. If the pick is bad, play moves to the next player. When one player has the 5 cards of a group, the player spreads them out. The winner is the one who completes and lays down the most groups.

LOCATING NORTH

Some constellations help you find your way at night. The constellation Ursa Major contains the Big Dipper, an asterism which is shaped like a saucepan; by taking the two stars opposite the handle and following the direction they suggest outward, you can find Polaris, the North Star. All you have to do then, is to find the shortest route between Polaris and the horizon to find due north.

THEY NEVER SET

In the northern latitudes (from 40°N latitude), Ursa Major, Ursa Minor, Draco, Cassiopeia, and Cepheus are visible all night from January to December. Astronomers call these constellations "circumpolar" because they are found in a circle above the horizon that has the North Star (Polaris) as its center, and as its radius, the distance from Polaris to the horizon. At the north pole, Polaris is at the zenith.

Cassiopeia

Big Dipper (part of Ursa Major)

Polaris

Little Dipper (part of Ursa Minor)

Cepheus

Draco (Dragon)

North

STARS OF ALL COLORS...

You can see yellow, red and blue stars with the naked eye. With binoculars, you will notice unusual shades of color, from emerald green to violet, through orange, lemon yellow, and bright red. These colors tell you about the temperature of the stars. In general, hot stars are blue, those that are cooler are mostly yellow, like the Sun, and those that are red are even cooler.

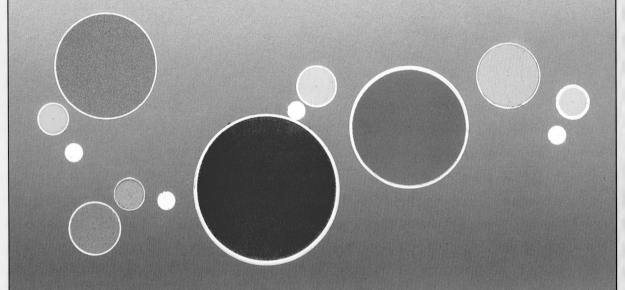

...AND OF ALL SIZES

In the last century, astronomers calculated the distance between us and stars visible to the naked eye. They realized that the Sun, which seems immense to us because it is right nearby, is, in fact, a little star. Vega, the blue star in Lyra, is four times larger, and Betelgeuse, the red star in Orion, is 400 times more massive than our Sun.

BUILD A MODEL OF THE BIG DIPPER

The Big Dipper is an *asterism* of Ursa Major, the Great Bear. An asterism is a noticeable pattern of stars that is part of one or more constellations.

The names of the stars and distances **1**, **2** and **3** are given on page 43. **1** and **2** are the distances on the x and y axis for each star. **3** is the length from the paper to the end of the stick.

• Measure distances **1** and **2** on graph paper for each star.

• Paste the paper to the bottom of the outside of a shoe box.

• Mark a line on each of the 7 sticks at the length of the distance **3**.

• Push each stick into the box so the distance you measured sticks out, and make them stay upright with balls of modeling clay inside and outside the box.

Look at the box from side x and draw an imaginary line between the straws; you will find the famous shape of the Big Dipper!

CONCLUSION

When you look at two stars that seem to you to be side by side in the sky, don't forget that they can be separated by an immense space. Even if they seem equally bright, it is entirely possible that a very little one is close to us and the other, a very big one, is very far off.

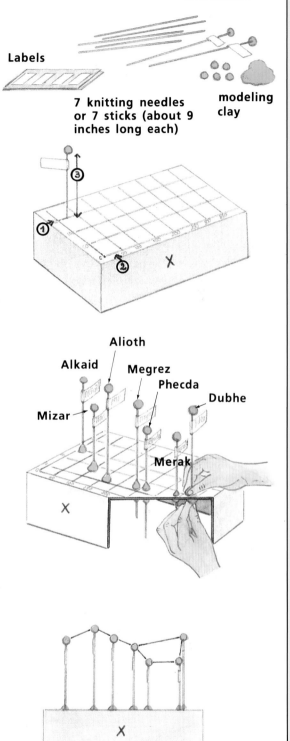

Labels

7 knitting needles or 7 sticks (about 9 inches long each)

modeling clay

Alkaid
Alioth
Megrez
Phecda
Dubhe
Mizar
Merak

THE MILKY WAY

While you're comfortably lying in a deck chair or stretched out on a blanket, you can study the night sky. From Perseus to Taurus, you journey through the constellations, which are now familiar to you. Your eye is drawn to a whitish trail that crosses the sky: the Milky Way. If you look through your binoculars, you will notice that it is composed of an irregular swarm of stars. The Milky Way is made up of hundreds of millions of stars. The Sun is but one among these millions, no bigger, no more beautiful, just one that is important to us because it allows us to exist.

The Milky Way, seen from above, resembles an immense wheel of fireworks. We can distinguish the central region and the arms that unwind around it.

Accompanied by its collection of planets, meteorites, and comets, the Sun takes 250 million years to make its way around the Milky Way. The Sun is located at the edge, in a location astronomers call the "Orion arm."

If this picture were actually done to scale, the solar system would be so small you could not see it. Its size is greatly exaggerated in the picture.

SOME STORIES

The ancients invented a thousand amazing legends to explain the presence of the Milky Way. For the Egyptians, the Milky Way and the stars were painted on the body of a goddess, who bent in a great arch around the Earth.

Certain African tribes thought the Milky Way was the spinal column of a gigantic animal that supported the sky and the stars.

For the Greeks, this white path came from the milk that fell from the breast of Hera, Zeus's wife, when she was nursing little Hercules. The milk flowed between the stars and formed a genuine road. In Greek, "milky way" was *galáxias*; this expression is at the root of the word "galaxy." The Milky Way is our galaxy.

VISIBLE ALL YEAR LONG

You can see the Milky Way in all seasons. On summer nights, the position of the Earth relative to the Sun makes us look toward the center of the galaxy, while in winter, our view is directed towards the outside. It is for this reason that the Milky Way seems much denser and brighter in summer than in winter. In the picture on pages 38–39, the Milky Way galaxy is seen from above. Here, you see it in profile. You can notice how fine the arms are and how the center is globe-shaped.

winter ← □ → summer

MILLIONS OF GALAXIES

In the 1920s, astronomers discovered that millions of other galaxies existed in the universe. Since then, they have grouped them by shape: barred spiral (like our own), spiral, spherical, elliptical, irregular.

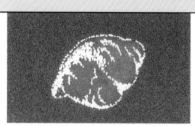

spherical galaxy

spiral galaxy

elliptical galaxy

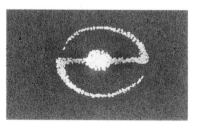

barred spiral galaxy

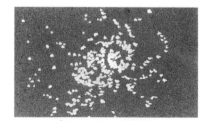

irregular galaxy

STAR CLUSTERS, NEBULAS, AND GALAXIES

While studying the Milky Way through your binoculars, try to identify the following formations:

Double stars. Two stars that rotate around one another. Some very beautiful ones are in the constellations Lyra, Cygnus, and Andromeda.

Globular cluster. Sometimes, stars are so bunched together that you need a strong telescope to distinguish them from each other. This is called a globular cluster. The star cluster in Hercules is one of the most beautiful.

Nebulas. It may seem there are large areas without stars in the Milky Way. In some areas, the stars are hidden behind gigantic clouds of dust and gas called nebulas.

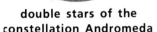

double stars of the constellation Andromeda   **open clusters of stars in Perseus**

Open cluster. In Taurus, Aquila, and Perseus, you can observe small bundles of stars which astronomers call "open clusters." In these formations, the stars are about the same distance from the Earth. The most famous is the open star cluster of the Pleiades.

Crab Nebula

Galaxies. Perhaps you will locate a small, blurry, elongated spot in the constellation Andromeda: this is another galaxy, made up of billions of stars, very far from ours.

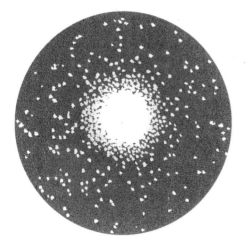

globular cluster in Hercules (Great Cluster)

Andromeda Galaxy

MEASUREMENTS FOR BUILDING A MODEL OF THE SOLAR SYSTEM*

| | Diameter | | | | Distance to the Sun | | | | Distance** with the same scale as the diameters | |
| | Model | | Actual | | Model | | Actual | | | |
	in	cm	mi	km	ft. in.	m	mi	km	mi	km
Mercury	2.7	5	2 783	4 480	7.9"	0.2	36	58	.3	0.5
Venus	7.7	12	7 705	12 400	15.7"	0.4	67	108	.7	1
Earth	7.9	12	7 926	12 756	19.7"	0.5	93	150	.9	1.5
Mars	4.2	7	4 225	6 800	2'7"	0.8	141	228	1.4	2.3
Jupiter	88.7	143	88 735	142 800	8'10"	2.7	483	778	4.8	7.8
Saturn	75.	121	75 065	120 800	16'4"	5	886	1 427	8.9	14.3
Uranus	31.6	50	31 567	50 800	32'10"	10	1 783	2 870	17.8	28.7
Neptune	30.8	49	30 796	49 560	49'2"	15	2 796	4 500	28	45
Pluto	1.4	2	1 429	2 300	65'7"	20	3 728	6 000	37.3	60
Sun	863.7	1 400	863 746	1 390 000	—		—		—	

*You can make your model using inches and feet or centimeters and meters.
**In this column, you can read the distance from the planets to the Sun if you apply the same scale for the diameters and distances, so: 1 centimeter = 1,000 kilometers.

MEASUREMENTS FOR BUILDING A MODEL OF THE BIG DIPPER*

Names of the stars in the Big Dipper	Distance #1		Distance #2		Distance #3 Length of the stick	
	in	mm	in	mm	in	mm
Alkaid	5⅞	150	⅞	22	7¼	185
Mizar	3⁷⁄₁₆	88	4³⁄₁₆	106	8¼	210
Alioth	2³⁄₁₆	55	6¼	159	7½	190
Megrez	2½	65	8⅞	223	6¾	171
Phecda	3⅛	80	9¹¹⁄₁₆	245	4½	117
Merak	3	76	14³⁄₁₆	347	4⅞	123
Dubhe	4⅛	105	14½	355	7½	189

*You can make your model using inches or millimeters.

THE 7 GROUPS FOR THE NORTHERN CONSTELLATIONS GAME

Orion's Hunt: Orion, the Hunter; Ophiuchus, the Serpent Bearer; Lepus, the Hare; Scorpius, the Scorpion; Canis Major, the Greater Dog.
Legend of Perseus: Perseus; Cepheus; Cassiopeia; Andromeda; Pegasus, the Winged Horse.
Big and Little: Ursa Major, the Big Bear; Ursa Minor, the Little Bear; Canis Minor, the Lesser Dog; Leo, the Lion; Leo Minor, the Lesser Lion.
In the Water: Delphinus, the Dolphin; Pisces, the Fish; Cetus, the Whale; Cancer, the Crab; Capricornus, the Sea Goat.
In the Air: Aquila, the Eagle; Cygnus, the Swan; Corvus, the Crow; Draco, the Dragon; Corona Borealis, the Northern Crown.
Characters: Hercules; Boötes, the Herdsman; Auriga, the Charioteer; Gemini, the Twins; Virgo, the Virgin.
Animals: Aries, the Ram; Lynx; Monoceros, the Unicorn; Serpens, the Serpent; Canes Venatici, the Hunting Dogs

GLOSSARY

Arms: the arms of a galaxy are the large strands that circle out from the center. Usually, they shelter many nebulas and stars in the making.

Asterism: a noticeable pattern of stars that makes up part of one or more constellations; not a constellation itself, for example, the Big Dipper.

Astral: of or relating to the stars.

Astronauts: men and women who travel into space are called astronauts.

Atmosphere: the layer of gases (like oxygen and carbon dioxide) that surrounds a planet. Earth's atmosphere contains the gas oxygen, which we need to breathe. The atmosphere around other planets contains other gases.

Celestial: of or relating to the sky.

Celestial equator: the intersection of the extended Earth's equator with the celestial sphere.

Celestial sphere: the apparent sphere of the heavens, seen from the Earth, on which all celestial bodies seem to be projected.

Circumpolar: when a star or constellation never disappears below the horizon, but remains visible all year long, it is said to be circumpolar.

Constellation: a group of stars that seemed to early astronomers to form a configuration in the sky. There are 88

constellations. The names of many of the constellations come from Greek and Roman mythology.

Crater: a circular rocky formation seen on the surface of the Moon and other bodies in the solar system. Volcanic craters result from volcanic activity and impact craters are produced by falling meteorites.

Day/night: as the Earth rotates about itself, its different regions are turned toward or away from the Sun. Day corresponds to the hours when the Sun is present in the sky, and night to the hours when it has set.

Eclipse: obscuring of the light from a celestial body by another body.

Ecliptic: (1) the apparent path of the Sun across the sky on the celestial sphere during the year. (2) the plane of the Earth's orbit projected onto the sky.

Equator: imaginary line that encircles the Earth at an equal distance from the two poles.

Equinox: the equinox is a period during which night and day are of the same length: 12 hours all over the Earth; the times when the Sun, traveling along the eclipic, intersects with the celestial equator.

Focal length: the distance between the principal plane of a lens and the place where it concentrates the rays of light passing through it (the focus).

Focus: (v.) to bring an optical system into focus. (n.) the state or place of sharpest imaging of an object you are observing through an instrument, the focal point.

Galaxy: an enormous group of stars, gas, and dust, held together by mutual gravitation; it often takes the shape of a wheel of fireworks.

Gaseous planets: the gaseous planets are Jupiter, Saturn, Uranus, and Neptune. They are massive and have thick atmospheres.

Inclination: the angle between the orbital plane of a planet and the plane of the ecliptic. The axis of rotation of the Earth is inclined 23.5 degrees (always in the same direction) relative to our planet's path about the Sun.

Leap year: the term for a year containing 366 days. This happens every four years.

Light year: the distance light travels through space in one year.

Mare (pl., *maria*). *Mare* is Latin for sea. A dark, smooth region on the Moon. Early astronomers thought they were seas.

Meridian: an imaginary north-south reference line linking the geographic poles of the Earth and the zenith of a location.

Nebula: large cloudy region of gas and dust in a galaxy, which appears hazy to our view. In some nebulas, new stars are forming.

Phases of the Moon: changes in the Moon's appearance during different times of the month, caused by varying illumination from the Sun. These include the full moon, the first quarter, the crescent moon, the new moon, and the third quarter.

Planets: celestial bodies that circle a star, which reflect its light. In our solar system, the planets are Mercury, Venus, Earth, Mars, Jupiter, Saturn, Uranus, Neptune, and Pluto.

Poles: by extending the rotational axis of the Earth toward the stars in our imagination, we can define a true (celestial) north pole and south pole. In the direction of true (celestial) north, a bright star called Polaris (the North Star) can be distinguished; there is no star indicating the exact south pole.

Probe: an apparatus sent near or to other parts of the solar system in order to photograph them and analyze their composition.

Satellite: an attendant body that revolves around another celestial body. Most of the planets have natural satellites, like a moon, circling them. Artificial satellites are manmade and are used, for example, to transmit television signals or telephone communications from one continent to another.

Seasons: the inclination of the Earth's rotational axis causes variations in the amount of warmth and light from the Sun received by the Earth. When this amount is large, it is summer; when it is very little, it is winter. Spring and autumn are the intermediary seasons.

Solstice: the summer solstice (June 21) is the longest day in the northern hemisphere. The winter solstice (December 21) is the shortest day. The day when the Sun has no apparent northward motion, and is at the position furthest north of the celestial equator, is the summer solstice. The day when the

Sun has no apparent southward motion, and is furthest south of the celestial equator, is the winter solstice.

Star: a gigantic self-luminous heavenly body that produces energy by nuclear reactions at its core. It is very hot and produces warmth and light.

Star cluster: stars are grouped in clusters containing several dozens to several thousand stars. Star clusters are "open" if you can separate the stars from one another and "closed" or "globular" when they are too close together to be distinguished individually.

Sundial: instrument used to determine the time by observing the direction of the shadow of a stick called a gnomon.

Terrestrial planets: the Earthlike planets Mercury, Venus, Earth, and Mars. They are relatively small and their atmospheres are not very thick.

Universal time (UT): Astronomers record any instant of time as it would be measured from the prime meridian in Greenwich, England. This is called universal time.

Zenith: a point on the celestial sphere directly over the head of the observer.